P9-DTT-979

SURVIVORS OF THE HOLOCAUST

TRUE STORIES OF SIX EXTRAORDINARY CHILDREN

EDITED BY KATH SHACKLETON ILLUSTRATED BY ZANE WHITTINGHAM

sourcebooks eXplore

First published in the United States in 2019 by Sourcebooks

Producer and editor
Kath Shackleton

Contributors
Heinz Skyte
Trude Silman
Martin Kapel
Ruth Rogoff
Arek Hersh
Suzanne Ripton

Illustrations
Zane Whittingham

Design and layout
Ryan Jones

Additional artwork
Laura Tattersfield
Oana Nechifor

Cover design © 2019 by Sourcebooks

Sourcebooks and the colophon are registered trademarks of Sourcebooks, Inc.

All rights reserved.

Every attempt has been made to clear copyright. Should there be any inadvertent omission please apply to the publisher for rectification.

Hand-drawn digital illustrations adapted from the original vector-based animation.

Published by Sourcebooks eXplore, an imprint of Sourcebooks Kids
P.O. Box 4410, Naperville, Illinois 60567–4410
(630) 961-3900
sourcebookskids.com

Originally published in 2016 in Great Britain by Franklin Watts, an imprint of Hachette Children's Group, part of the Watts Publishing Group.

Library of Congress Cataloging-in-Publication Data is on file with the publisher.

Source of Production: RR Donnelley Asia Printing Solutions, Ltd., Dongguan, Guangdong Province, China
Date of Production: July 2019
Run Number: 5015095

Printed and bound in China.
RRD 10 9 8 7 6 5 4 3 2 1

Foreword

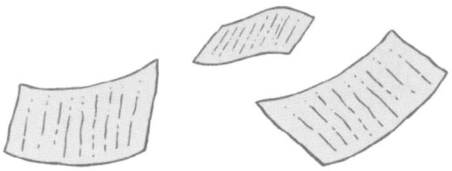

Each story you will read in this book is a true account of what happened to six young people over seventy years ago. Heinz, Trude, Ruth, Martin, Suzanne, and Arek lived at home with their families. They went to school, enjoyed friendships, had hobbies, and hopes for the future. Then one day their lives changed forever. They had done nothing wrong. They were born into Jewish families, and they were persecuted for this reason alone: they were Jewish.

From 1933 onwards, Nazi Germany introduced new anti-Semitic racial measures, which became law in 1935—the Nuremberg Laws. These laws prevented Jewish people from being citizens of Germany and forbade marriage between Jewish and non-Jewish people. Gradually, all their rights were removed.

On the night of November 9th, 1938, synagogues, homes, and businesses owned by Jewish people were attacked and set on fire. This is known as "Kristallnacht," or the Night of Broken Glass. Some thirty thousand Jewish men were arrested and sent to concentration camps. As Nazi Germany occupied the rest of Europe during the Second World War, their racial policies were implemented across the whole of their new territory, including what was then Czechoslovakia, Poland, Holland, Belgium, Greece, Hungary, and France. This led to the Holocaust, during which six million Jewish men, women, and children were systematically murdered.

I have known Trude, Ruth, Martin, Heinz, Arek, and Suzanne for many years. They are an inspiration to people who hear their stories in person. They all lost their country, their families, their culture, and their right to exist simply because they were Jewish.

Today they live in Leeds. They have overcome adversity, made new lives and new families, but they never forget their past. They know they are the lucky ones who escaped or were liberated, but they never forget those who did not.

It is not easy for them to tell their stories. They agreed to because they want people to know what can happen when people are subjected to discrimination and persecution for being seen as "different." Their dearest wish is that no one should suffer as they did and that people should never again stand by when injustice is taking place. It is their belief that we are all part of the human race and we should always respect each other and our differences. We hope by reading these stories, you will be able to think about your own lives and how you can make a difference for a better world today.

Lilian Black

Chair, Holocaust Survivors'
Friendship Association

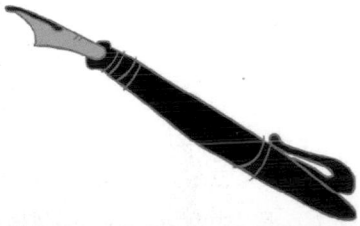

Contents

Heinz's story 5
Trude's story 19
Ruth's story 33
Martin's story 45
Suzanne's story 61
Arek's story 75

What Happened Next? 90
Glossary 92
Timeline 94
Index and websites 96

HEINZ'S STORY

I REMEMBER THE DAY THAT THE NAZIS CAME TO POWER.
I WAS ALMOST 13.
I REMEMBER LOOKING DOWN FROM OUR WINDOW IN FUERTH, NUREMBERG.
CRACKLE
CRACKLE
CRACKLE
CRACKLE
THE NAZIS ALWAYS CELEBRATED THEIR SUCCESSES BY TORCHLIGHT PROCESSIONS.
AND THEY MARCHED PAST AND SANG SONGS, BLOODTHIRSTY SONGS.

THE NUREMBERG LAWS THAT CAME IN THE AUTUMN OF 1935 LEGALIZED ANTI-JEWISH MEASURES.
Jude
WE WERE NO LONGER ALLOWED TO GO TO CINEMAS AND THEATERS AND BE MEMBERS OF CLUBS.
AS A CHILD OF ANY AGE, TO BE EXCLUDED FROM YOUR PEERS IS A BLOW.
YOU FEEL INFERIOR...
...AND YOU QUESTION YOUR EXISTENCE.
CRACK!

THERE WERE THREE JEWISH BOYS, INCLUDING ME, LEFT IN OUR CLASS.
THE MAIN HITLER YOUTH LEADER CAME AND SAID,
It's time you left the school. We don't want you here!
THUMP!
I LEFT SCHOOL AT 16.

AT THE AGE OF 18, I WENT TO COLLEGE IN HAMBURG TO LEARN ENGLISH.

BACK IN NUREMBERG, MY PARENTS WERE ARRESTED, ROUNDED UP, AND KEPT STANDING IN THE SQUARE IN THE CENTER OF THE TOWN FOR ABOUT TWO HOURS.
CLICK
CLICK
THEY WERE ABUSED, SPAT UPON.
CLICK
CLICK
CLICK
RUN!
THE SYNAGOGUE WAS SET ON FIRE. THE WOMEN, THE OLDER PEOPLE, AND THE CHILDREN WERE SENT HOME.

WHEN MY MOTHER GOT HOME, ABOUT FOUR O'CLOCK IN THE MORNING, SHE RANG WHERE I WAS STAYING. SHE SAID,
Father's gone away.
WHICH WAS CODE FOR "HE'S BEEN ARRESTED."
OOOFFF!
You get dressed, go for a walk. Now!

SO THAT'S WHAT I DID.
I SAT ON PARK BENCHES...
...THEN I WENT AROUND THE DEPARTMENT STORES.
I TRIED TO MAKE MYSELF SMALL, NOT TO STAND OUT.
TAP
TAP
CLICK
CLICK
CLICK
TAP
TAP
TAP
I COULD SEE THE SMOKE FROM THE BURNING SYNAGOGUES EVERYWHERE.

I COULD ALSO SEE GROUPS OF JEWISH PEOPLE BEING FROGMARCHED THROUGH THE STREETS AFTER THEY'D BEEN ARRESTED.

MOMMY!

WINDOWS WERE SMASHED.

CRACK!

THE GERMANS INVENTED THE TERM...

KRISTALLNACHT

...BECAUSE OF ALL THE BROKEN GLASS.

EVENTUALLY I WENT HOME. THE LANDLADY SAID, "THE GESTAPO HAVE BEEN LOOKING FOR YOU." IT'S A GOOD THING THAT I DID LEAVE THE DIGS, OTHERWISE I WOULD HAVE BEEN SENT TO A CONCENTRATION CAMP.
BANG
BANG
BANG
FATHER WAS ARRESTED AND THEN SENT TO DACHAU CONCENTRATION CAMP NEAR MUNICH.
HE WAS THERE FOR FIVE OR SIX WEEKS.
MOST OF THE PEOPLE WERE RELEASED JUST BEFORE CHRISTMAS 1938.
FATHER CAME HOME AND WAS A COMPLETELY CHANGED MAN.

IT WAS THEN QUITE OBVIOUS THAT THERE WAS NO FUTURE FOR US IN GERMANY.
BRUSH
BRUSH
BRUSH
BRUSH
BRUSH
BRUSH
THERE WAS NOWHERE FOR US TO GO. NO COUNTRY WANTED US.
SWISH
SWISH
SWISH
SWISH
FRANK, MY BROTHER, WAS IN LEEDS.
HE TRIED VERY HARD TO GET ME A TRAINEE POST AND FINALLY SUCCEEDED...
Leeds
Hamburg
GREAT BRITAIN
GERMANY
...AND I CAME TO LEEDS.

DEUTSCHES REICH
J
REISEPASS
DEUTSCHES REICH
J
REISEPASS
WE MANAGED TO GET VISAS FOR OUR PARENTS EVENTUALLY. AND THEY CAME, THANK GOD, BECAUSE FOUR DAYS LATER...
BANG!
BANG!
BOOM!
BOOM!
...WAR BROKE OUT.
BOOM!

THE DAY WAR BROKE OUT, A POLICEMAN CAME, ASKING US TO COME DOWN AND REPORT TO POLICE HEADQUARTERS.

I WAS REGISTERED AS AN...

ENEMY ALIEN

CAMERAS AND BINOCULARS WERE IMPOUNDED. THEY WERE CONSIDERED SPYING EQUIPMENT.

EIGHT MONTHS LATER, WINSTON CHURCHILL BECAME PRIME MINISTER AND HIS CIVIL SERVANTS FAMOUSLY ASKED HIM,

What shall we do with these enemy aliens?

Collar the lot!

SO WE WERE INTERNED, FATHER, BROTHER, AND ME.
BANG!
BANG!
BANG!
ALL OF US FELT A BIT ANGRY, BECAUSE WE WERE MORE OPPOSED TO THE NAZIS THAN THE NATIVE BRITISH WERE.

HEINZ AND HIS BROTHER FRANK WERE SENT TO INTERNMENT CAMPS IN CANADA FOR TWO YEARS. THEY NEVER DID GET THEIR CHANCE TO FIGHT THE NAZIS.

TRUDE'S STORY

I'M BACK IN MY SCHOOL DAYS IN CZECHOSLOVAKIA, ABOUT 1938.
I HAVE A WONDERFUL PHOTOGRAPH, A CLASS PHOTOGRAPH OF ALL OF US.
IT'S SOMETHING THAT IS A GREAT PLEASURE TO LOOK AT, BUT IT IS ALSO EXTREMELY SAD...
...BECAUSE UNFORTUNATELY, THE GERMANS KILLED MANY, MANY CHILDREN.

ONE AND A HALF MILLION INNOCENT CHILDREN WERE KILLED DURING THE HOLOCAUST.
AND WHEN I LOOK AT THESE FACES, I DON'T KNOW WHO SURVIVED AND WHO DIDN'T.
I ONLY KNOW THAT I SURVIVED.
WHY SHOULD INNOCENT PEOPLE, JUST BECAUSE THEY WERE JEWISH, BE KILLED FOR NO REASON AT ALL?

WE HAD THIS RADIO IN OUR DINING ROOM, AND FATHER WAS OFTEN LISTENING.
BUT WHEN HE HAD THE NEWS ON, YOU COULD HEAR THIS SHOUTING.
@!!*#
AND THAT, OF COURSE, WAS THE TYPICAL HITLER SPEECH-MAKING.
!%#!!!@
STOMP
STOMP
STOMP
STOMP
STOMP

EVERYBODY WAS AFRAID OF THIS KNOCK AT THE DOOR, AND IT ALWAYS CAME DURING THE NIGHT...
...WHEN THEY CAME TO TAKE PEOPLE AWAY, EITHER TO BEAT THEM UP OR WHATEVER...
...AND THAT FEAR WAS THERE ALL THE TIME I WAS AT HOME.

YOU FEEL INSECURE. YOU DON'T FEEL AT EASE.
YOU CAN'T RELAX, AND YOU KNOW THAT SOMETHING IS WRONG.

THE GERMANS DIDN'T COME INTO CZECHOSLOVAKIA UNTIL MARCH 15TH, 1939.
BOOM!

I REALIZED THAT MY PARENTS WANTED TO GET THE OTHER CHILDREN AWAY TO SAFETY.

THEN MY TURN CAME. I LEFT HOME ON MARCH 28TH, 1939.

THE ONLY THING I REMEMBER IS GETTING INTO A TAXI.
I REMEMBER MY MOTHER AND MY FATHER AND MY BROTHER STANDING NEAR ME. BUT I CANNOT REMEMBER SAYING GOODBYE TO THEM.
I CAN'T REMEMBER WHETHER I HUGGED THEM, KISSED THEM, WHETHER I CRIED.
I HAVE ABSOLUTELY NO RECOLLECTION WHATSOEVER.

I STARTED GETTING HOMESICK AND I STARTED FEELING VERY, VERY POORLY.

BECAUSE A) I WAS MISSING MY PARENTS AND...
ahoj!
...B) I DIDN'T SPEAK ONE WORD OF ENGLISH.
Porridge Oats
Marmalade
THE FOOD WAS TOTALLY DIFFERENT. I'D NEVER EATEN TOAST, PORRIDGE, KIPPERS, MARMALADE...ALL OF THESE NORMAL ENGLISH THINGS.

AND I JUST BASICALLY CRIED FOR AS LONG AS I STAYED WITH THEM.
SOON, I MOVED ON. FROM THE AGE OF NINE, I LIVED WITH SO MANY DIFFERENT PEOPLE.
IN THOSE FOUR YEARS, IN THOSE WAR YEARS, I WOULD THINK I MUST HAVE BEEN THROUGH AT LEAST 15 TO 20 DIFFERENT PLACES.
I NEVER SAW MY PARENTS AFTER MARCH 28TH, 1939.

FATHER WAS DEPORTED TO A NAZI CONCENTRATION CAMP CALLED AUSCHWITZ IN POLAND...
...ON APRIL 19TH, 1942.
AND BY MAY 8TH, 1942, HE HAD BEEN KILLED.

THE LAST PROPER EVIDENCE I HAVE THAT MY MOTHER WAS ALIVE...
...WAS WHEN SHE WAS TRANSPORTED TO A SMALL CONCENTRATION CAMP NEAR BRATISLAVA CALLED SERED.
AND I'VE BEEN WORKING FOR YEARS AND YEARS TO TRY AND TRACE HER...
...AND I'M ALMOST AT THE END OF THE TRAIL.

I RECEIVED SOME EVIDENCE FROM A TESTIMONY GIVEN BY SOMEBODY IN 1962...
...WHO COULD HAVE BEEN ON THE SAME TRANSPORT THAT MY MOTHER WAS TAKEN ON...

...AND ON A DEATH MARCH ON WHICH SHE WOULD HAVE BEEN SHOT AND KILLED.

TRUDE EVENTUALLY SETTLED WELL IN A BOARDING SCHOOL IN CORNWALL. SHE STUDIED HARD AND WENT ON TO UNIVERSITY.

RUTH'S STORY

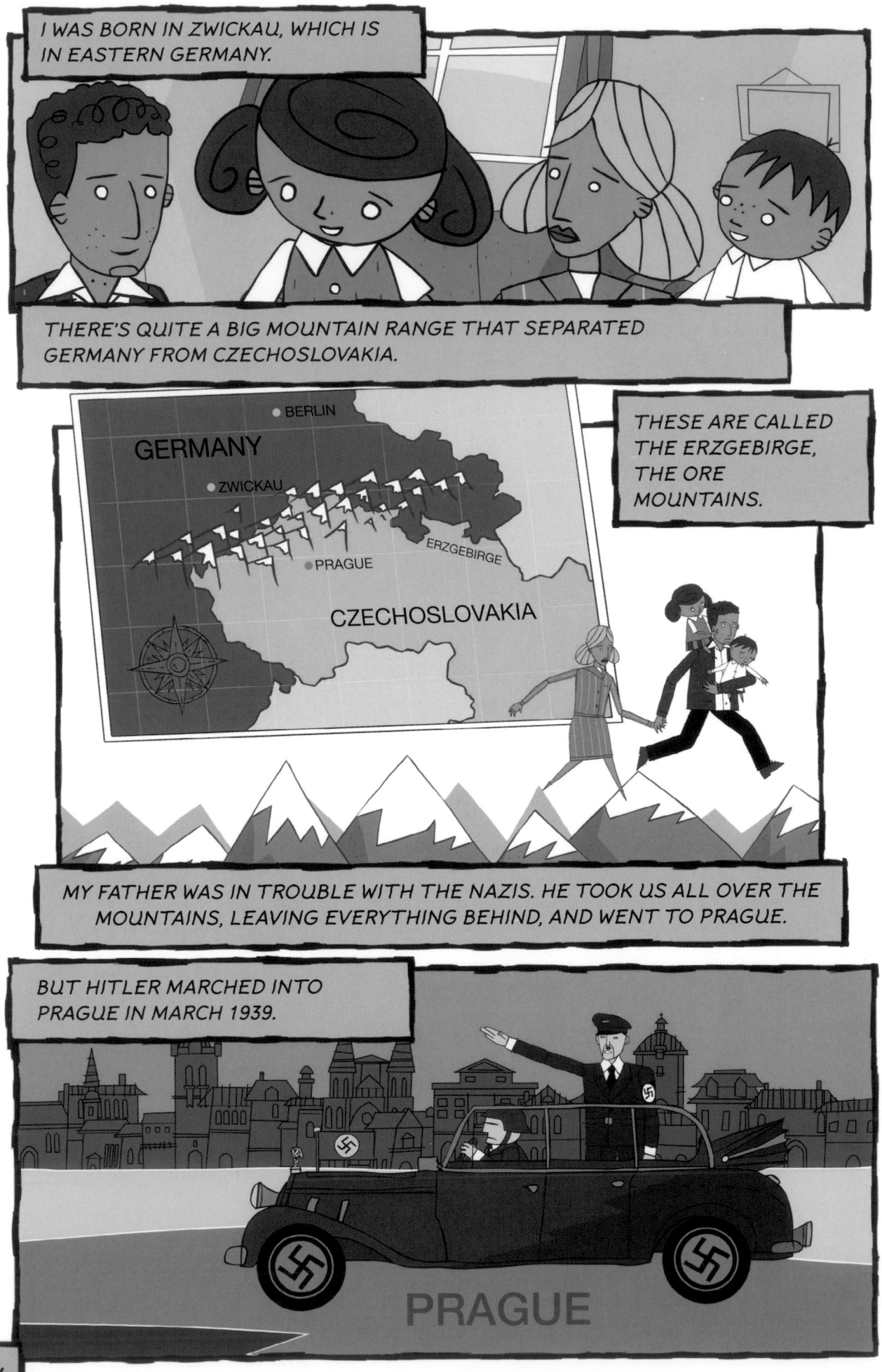
I WAS BORN IN ZWICKAU, WHICH IS IN EASTERN GERMANY.
THERE'S QUITE A BIG MOUNTAIN RANGE THAT SEPARATED GERMANY FROM CZECHOSLOVAKIA.
BERLIN
GERMANY
ZWICKAU
ERZGEBIRGE
PRAGUE
CZECHOSLOVAKIA
THESE ARE CALLED THE ERZGEBIRGE, THE ORE MOUNTAINS.
MY FATHER WAS IN TROUBLE WITH THE NAZIS. HE TOOK US ALL OVER THE MOUNTAINS, LEAVING EVERYTHING BEHIND, AND WENT TO PRAGUE.
BUT HITLER MARCHED INTO PRAGUE IN MARCH 1939.
PRAGUE

MY FATHER REALIZED HE WAS STILL ON A NAZI WANTED LIST...
...SO HE LEFT MY MOTHER AND WENT TO POLAND.
IT WAS EXTREMELY DIFFICULT FOR MY MOTHER TO BE LEFT ALONE WITH TWO SMALL CHILDREN.
SPLAT
STREET BY STREET, JEWS WERE CLEARED...
...AND ANY MOMENT IT WAS PROBABLY OUR TURN.
MY MOTHER...SHE MUST HAVE HAD A WILL OF IRON AND GREAT COURAGE.

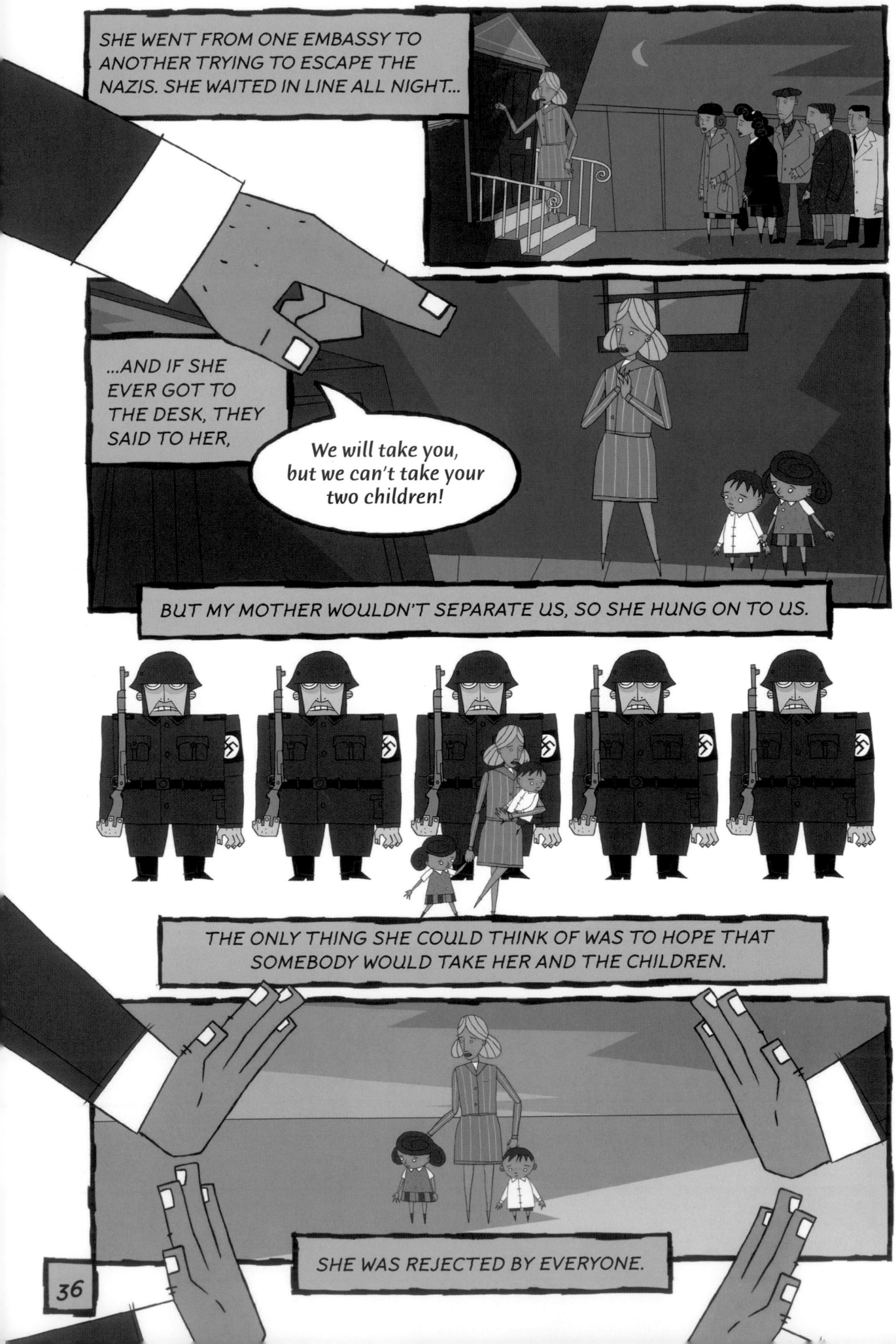
SHE WENT FROM ONE EMBASSY TO ANOTHER TRYING TO ESCAPE THE NAZIS. SHE WAITED IN LINE ALL NIGHT...
...AND IF SHE EVER GOT TO THE DESK, THEY SAID TO HER,
We will take you, but we can't take your two children!
BUT MY MOTHER WOULDN'T SEPARATE US, SO SHE HUNG ON TO US.
THE ONLY THING SHE COULD THINK OF WAS TO HOPE THAT SOMEBODY WOULD TAKE HER AND THE CHILDREN.
SHE WAS REJECTED BY EVERYONE.

BUT THEN, THE MIRACLE HAPPENED.

...BECAUSE WE OPENED THE DOOR TO A WOMAN FROM THE BRITISH EMBASSY WHO HAD BRAVED THE CURFEW.

SHE BROUGHT US AN ENTRY VISA TO BRITAIN, TRAIN TICKETS TO GET THROUGH GERMANY, THROUGH HOLLAND...
VISA
GREAT BRITAIN
...AND A FERRY TICKET TO RAMSGATE.
BUT THE EMBASSY LADY DID NOT HAVE AN EXIT VISA. YOU WERE SUPPOSED TO HAVE AN EXIT VISA TO CROSS BORDERS.
AND SHE SAID,
You'll just have to say you're going to see family in Holland.
Take nothing with you that could possibly show anyone that you're going for more than one day.

GERMANY
CZECHOSLOVAKIA
PRAGUE
WE MADE IT THROUGH CZECHOSLOVAKIA WITHOUT ANY PROBLEM, AND WE GOT ON THE TRAIN IN GERMANY.

WE SAT DOWN, THINKING,
Good, we've got a carriage to ourselves.
THEN A NAZI SS OFFICER CAME AND SAT NEXT TO MY MOTHER. HE WAS TRYING TO FLIRT WITH HER.

THE FACT THAT HE SAT THERE...NOW THAT MIGHT HAVE BEEN HER SALVATION, AS THE GUARDS DIDN'T ASK FOR HER PAPERS.

OFF WE WENT TO THE HOOK OF HOLLAND AND GOT ON A FERRY TO RAMSGATE.
GREAT BRITAIN
RAMSGATE
ON THE FERRY, I KEPT SAYING,
When are we going to be in England?
When it starts raining, you'll know you're in England.
MY MOTHER GOT REALLY FED UP WITH ME!
AS I WAS ON THE TRAIN, IT BEGAN RAINING...
...AND I MUST HAVE BEEN THE ONLY PERSON THERE WHO WAS JUST TOTALLY THRILLED, BECAUSE I KNEW I WAS IN ENGLAND.
ENGLAND
SPLASH
SPLASH

THE NEXT MORNING WAS SUNDAY, SEPTEMBER 3RD, 1939.
LIVERPOOL STREET STATION
G E R
AS WE ARRIVED AT LIVERPOOL STREET STATION...
...I PUT MY FOOT ON THE PLATFORM.
SUDDENLY, EVERYTHING WENT QUIET AND THERE WAS AN ANNOUNCEMENT ON THE LOUDSPEAKER.
AND EVERYBODY STOOD PERFECTLY STILL.

THE ANNOUNCEMENT WAS THE BRITISH PRIME MINISTER NEVILLE CHAMBERLAIN SAYING,
I am speaking to you from the Cabinet Room at 10 Downing Street.
This morning, the British Ambassador in Berlin handed the German government a final note...
...stating that unless we heard from them by 11 o'clock, saying they were prepared at once to withdraw their troops from Poland...
3924

...a state of war would exist between us.
I have to tell you now, that no such undertaking has been received...
...and that consequently, this country is at war with Germany.
BOOM!
BANG!
BOOM!

RUTH'S WHOLE FAMILY WAS REUNITED SHORTLY AFTER THEIR ARRIVAL IN LONDON. THEY WERE LUCKY TO BE ALIVE.

MARTIN'S STORY

IN 1938, WHEN I WAS EIGHT YEARS OLD...
...THERE OCCURRED WHAT HAS BECOME KNOWN AS THE "POLENAKTION."
POLAND
EARLY IN THE MORNING, WE WERE ALL SLEEPING IN OUR BEDS IN OUR HOME IN GERMANY. THE NAZIS ENTERED OUR FLAT.
WE WERE GOING TO BE TAKEN AWAY.

WE WERE PUT ON BOARD A TRAIN.
WE CAME TO REALIZE THAT THE PASSENGERS WERE ALL POLISH JEWS.
WE WERE LUCKIER THAN SOME. WE HAD BEEN TAKEN AS AN ENTIRE FAMILY.

SOME OF THE FAMILIES HAD BEEN SEPARATED. THEY DIDN'T KNOW WHETHER THEY WERE EVER GOING TO SEE ONE ANOTHER EVER AGAIN.
TO MAKE MATTERS WORSE, THERE WERE PEOPLE OF ALL AGES...
WAAA!
...BABIES...
...THERE WERE VERY OLD PEOPLE...
AND PEOPLE WHO WERE ILL. SOME HAD BEEN TAKEN OUT OF HOSPITAL BEDS.

WE TRAVELED FOR THE REST OF THE DAY, AND AFTER IT GOT DARK...
POLAND
GERMANY
...THE TRAIN STOPPED AND WE WERE TOLD TO GET OFF.
OUTSIDE THE STATION...
...THERE WERE TWO ROWS OF SS MEN.
WE WERE MARCHED OFF, AND THE RUMOR WENT AROUND THAT WE WERE BEING TAKEN TO SOME REMOTE PLACE...
BANG!
...WHERE WE WOULD ALL BE SHOT.

I SAW PEOPLE COLLAPSE FROM EXHAUSTION, AND I WAS LEFT IN NO DOUBT ABOUT THE BRUTALITY OF THESE SS MEN.
WE MARCHED FOR HOURS....
...AND THEN WE WERE STOPPED AT A RAILWAY LINE, AND WE WERE TOLD THAT THE SS MEN WERE NOT COMING ANY FARTHER.

IT SEEMS LIKELY THAT THIS WAS IN FACT...
POLAND
...THE POLISH FRONTIER.
CLICK
CLICK
THE SS MEN WOULDN'T WANT TO CROSS THAT AT THIS PARTICULAR TIME.
THAT COULD PROVOKE AN INTERNATIONAL INCIDENT.
CLICK
CLICK
WE WERE TOLD THAT WE WOULD HAVE TO GO ON MARCHING BETWEEN THE RAILS.

ON EITHER SIDE THERE WERE DITCHES, AND ANYBODY WHO FELL RISKED INJURY...
...NOT ONLY FROM THE FALL...
...BUT ALSO FROM BEING TRAMPLED.

SOME HOURS LATER, ARMED POLICE AND SOLDIERS CAME ALONG—POLISH SOLDIERS, THAT IS—AND OF COURSE THEY HAD KNOWN NOTHING OF OUR COMING.
POLAND

THE POLISH AUTHORITIES DID TRY TO FORCE SOME PEOPLE BACK INTO GERMANY.
POLAND
THE GERMAN AUTHORITIES WERE READY FOR THAT, AND POLISH ATTEMPTS TO SEND PEOPLE BACK TO GERMANY FAILED.
BUT WE MANAGED TO GET TO KRAKÓW IN POLAND WHERE WE HAD SOME RELATIVES...
...AND WE ARRIVED ON THEIR DOORSTEP.

ABOUT THE TIME THAT WE WENT TO POLAND, BRITAIN ALLOWED SOME JEWISH CHILDREN TO BE BROUGHT OVER FROM EUROPE, IN WHAT BECAME KNOWN AS THE "KINDERTRANSPORT."
GREAT BRITAIN
GERMANY
POLAND
FRANCE
MY SISTER AND I WERE VERY LUCKY TO BE AMONG THE FEW CHILDREN TO BE RESCUED FROM POLAND.
Name
Sex Male
Place
WE WOULD HAVE DIED WITH THE REST OF OUR FAMILY IF WE HADN'T BEEN RESCUED.

WE WENT TO FOSTER PARENTS IN COVENTRY IN ENGLAND.
IN THE AUTUMN OF 1940, THE SO-CALLED BLITZ BEGAN.
COVENTRY WAS ONE OF THE MOST SEVERELY BOMBED CITIES.
WE HAD 17 RAIDS WHEN A FEW BOMBS WERE DROPPED ON THE CITY.
AND THEN ONE NIGHT, WE HAD A VERY BIG RAID.

THE HOME OFFICE ADVICE WAS THAT IF YOU DIDN'T HAVE AN AIR-RAID SHELTER, THE SAFEST PART OF THE HOUSE WAS UNDER THE STAIRS.
UNDER OUR STAIRS WE HAD A SMALL PANTRY, SO WE ALL CROWDED INTO THAT, MY SISTER AND I...
...OUR FOSTER PARENTS...
...AND THE DOG.
THE DOG WAS VICIOUS. HE BIT QUITE A FEW PEOPLE. WE TRIED TO KEEP OUR DISTANCE.
BUT WHENEVER A BOMB CAME VERY NEAR, THE DOG GROWLED AND WE WERE REALLY AFRAID, ALL OF US.

WE HEARD A VERY LOUD HISSING SOUND...
...AND IT WAS OBVIOUS THAT THE BOMB WAS COMING NEAR.
IT LANDED JUST A FEW DOORS DOWN.

THE NEXT MORNING, WHEN WE EMERGED, OUR HOUSE HAD LOST ITS DOORS AND ITS WINDOWS AND PART OF THE ROOF.
IT'S AMAZING THAT THERE WERE MANY SMALL AIR RAIDS...
CARROTS 1D each
...AND GENERALLY SPEAKING, PEOPLE TOOK THEM IN STRIDE.

BOTH MARTIN AND HIS SISTER SURVIVED THE BOMBINGS IN COVENTRY, AND SETTLED WELL INTO THEIR NEW LIVES IN ENGLAND.

SUZANNE'S STORY

OOH, MY PARIS WAS GORGEOUS. I LIVED IN THE 20TH ARRONDISSEMENT.
I LOVED PARIS. BEING A LITTLE GIRL THERE WAS FUN.
WE USED TO WALK ALONG THE SEINE AND OVER THE BRIDGES.

Yippee!
MY MOM USED TO PUT ME ON A CAROUSEL RIDE.
WE WATCHED MARIONETTES IN THE PARK. THERE WAS ALWAYS MUSIC PLAYING.
IT WAS A LOVELY LIFE. IT WAS A CULTURED LIFE.
I REMEMBER GOING TO A PRESCHOOL.
A B C
I LOVED GOING THERE. BUT I DIDN'T GO THERE FOR VERY LONG.

SLOWLY, SLOWLY, MY LIFE CHANGED.
THE FIRST THING WE COULDN'T DO WAS WE COULDN'T GO OUT.
YOU STARTED TO HEAR NOISES THAT YOU HADN'T HEARD BEFORE. IT WAS REALLY SCARY SOMETIMES.
AS I UNDERSTAND IT NOW, WE WERE OCCUPIED, AND ALL OF THE SHOUTING AND ACTIVITY YOU COULD HEAR OUTSIDE WERE NAZI SOLDIERS.

THE DAY IT HAPPENED, IT WAS AUGUST AND IT WAS HOT.
I WAS WITH MY FATHER AT THE WINDOW, AND SUDDENLY HE SAID,
They're here!

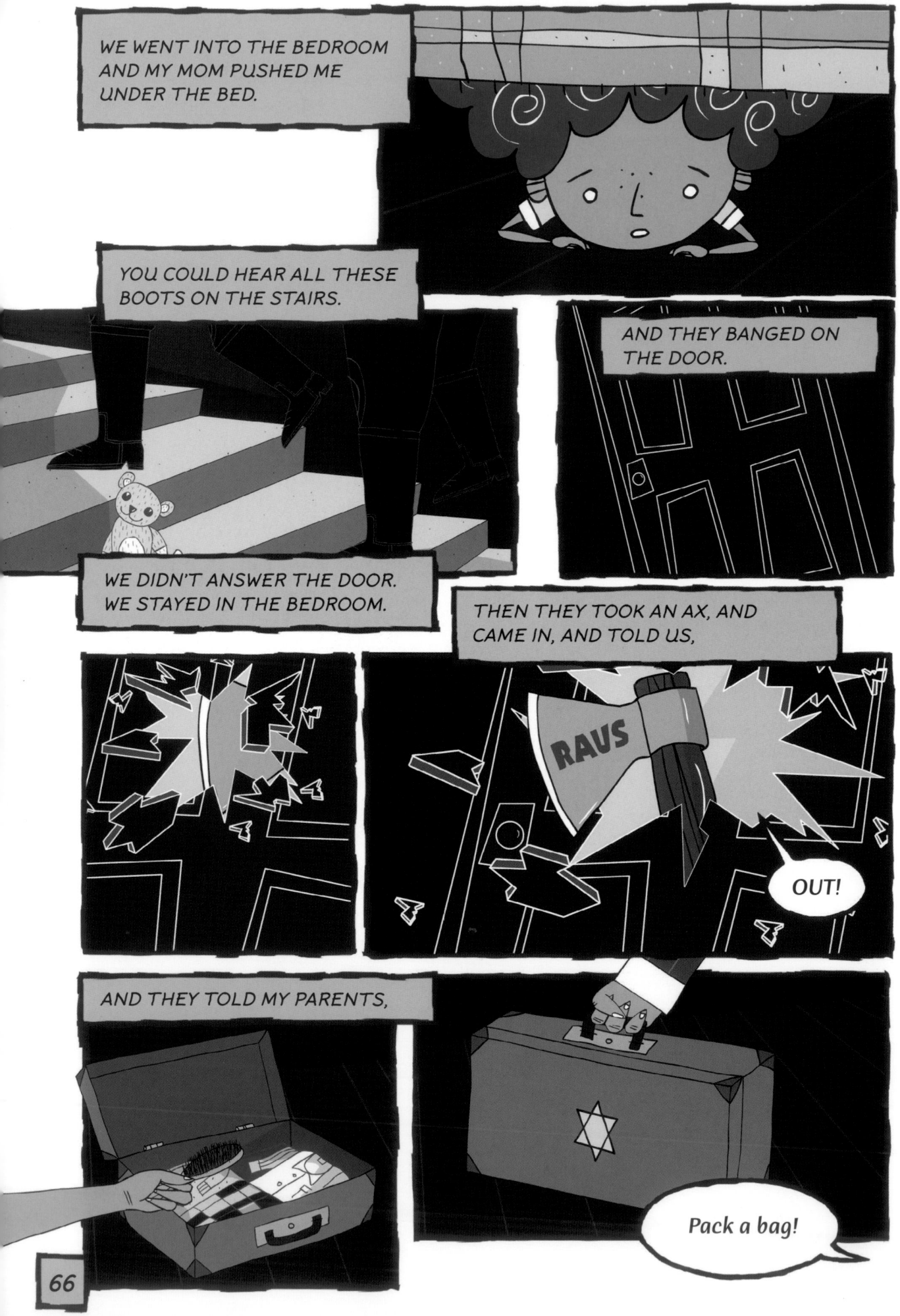
WE WENT INTO THE BEDROOM AND MY MOM PUSHED ME UNDER THE BED.
YOU COULD HEAR ALL THESE BOOTS ON THE STAIRS.
AND THEY BANGED ON THE DOOR.
WE DIDN'T ANSWER THE DOOR. WE STAYED IN THE BEDROOM.
THEN THEY TOOK AN AX, AND CAME IN, AND TOLD US,
RAUS
OUT!
AND THEY TOLD MY PARENTS,
Pack a bag!

DURING ALL THE COMMOTION, MADAME COLLOMB CAME IN.
SHE WAS OUR NEXT-DOOR NEIGHBOR.
What's my child doing in this apartment?
SHE TOOK MY HAND, AND TOOK ME AWAY.
HAD THEY REALIZED WHAT SHE WAS DOING, WE'D HAVE ALL BEEN SHOT ON THE SPOT. BUT SHE GOT AWAY WITH IT.

SHE TOOK ME TO HER APARTMENT AND PUT ME UNDERNEATH HER DINING TABLE, WITH A BIG CHENILLE TABLECLOTH OVER IT.
SHE MADE ME A LITTLE BED, AND I LIVED THERE FOR TWO OR THREE WEEKS.
IT WAS SOLITARY, AND IT WAS LONELY AND IT WAS DARK.
I HAD NIGHTMARES THERE.
I NEVER SAW MY PARENTS AGAIN AFTER THAT.
AND I WAS LOST, A TOTALLY LOST CHILD.

AFTER THAT, MADAME COLLOMB TOOK ME OUT ONE NIGHT, AND FURTIVELY WE HAD TO GO CATCH A TRAIN.
THE FIRST HIDING PLACE SHE TOOK ME TO WAS MONDOUBLEAU, WHICH IS SOUTHWEST OF PARIS.
MONDOUBLEAU
I COULDN'T GO TO SCHOOL. I COULDN'T GO OUT ON THE STREET BECAUSE THERE WERE GERMAN SOLDIERS EVERYWHERE.

THEY HID ME IN A SORT OF STRANGE OUTHOUSE.
I STAYED THERE FOR TWO YEARS IN HIDING.
THEN I WAS TAKEN TO THE AUVERGNE, TO A FARM IN THE MIDDLE OF NOWHERE. THERE WAS NO ELECTRICITY, NO WATER.
CLUCK
CLUCK
CLUCK
YOU HAD TO BE SELF-SUFFICIENT. YOU GREW UP OVERNIGHT.

I SLEPT OCCASIONALLY INSIDE THE HOUSE...
SPLASH
SPLASH

...BUT THEN OTHER TIMES I WENT AND SLEPT WITH THE GOAT...

...BECAUSE SHE'D HAD SOME KIDS.
THEY WERE WARM AND THEY WERE FRIENDLY AND THEY WOULD SNUFFLE AGAINST YOUR CHEEK.

DURING THE DAY I HAD TO GO OUT AND WORK LIKE A MAN.
CHOP
IT WAS HARD IN THE WINTER WHEN IT WAS FROZEN.
MY HANDS WERE BLUE AND THEY WERE CRACKED AND BLEEDING AND SORE...
...AND MY FEET WERE IN THE SAME CONDITION, BECAUSE I DIDN'T HAVE SHOES.
I USED TO SIT DOWN AND CRY SOMETIMES, BUT IT DIDN'T DO ANY GOOD, SO I STOPPED DOING THAT.
NOBODY HEARD.

NOBODY EVER SAID, "I'LL EXPLAIN WHAT HAPPENED TO YOU."
"I WILL EXPLAIN WHAT WAR MEANS."
"I WILL EXPLAIN WHAT HAPPENED TO YOUR PARENTS, THAT YOU ARE NEVER GOING TO SEE THEM AGAIN."
AAAHHH!
"I WILL EXPLAIN THAT YOU ARE NEVER GOING BACK TO YOUR HOUSE IN PARIS."
Paris.
Rue-de-Belleville.
"FORGET IT. IT'S GONE."

THE WAR ENDED IN 1945,
AND I WAS STILL IN THE AUVERGNE FOR TWO YEARS.
WE DIDN'T KNOW. WE HADN'T BEEN TOLD.

I DIDN'T KNOW THE WAR WAS OVER, BECAUSE WE DIDN'T HAVE NEWSPAPERS.

WE DIDN'T HAVE A RADIO, WE DIDN'T HAVE ELECTRICITY, NOBODY KNEW.

SUZANNE WAS EVENTUALLY RESCUED BY THE RED CROSS AND TAKEN TO LIVE WITH HER GRANDMOTHER IN NEWCASTLE, ENGLAND.

AREK'S STORY

I WAS BORN IN SIERADZ IN POLAND. ONE DAY, WHEN I WAS 15, THE NAZIS CAME AND TOOK US AWAY.
IN THE WAGON THERE WAS ONLY ONE VERY SMALL WINDOW.

IT WAS HOT.
WE WERE SO CRAMPED...
I'm so thirsty!
...WE COULDN'T EVEN SIT DOWN.

AAAHHH!!
SOME PEOPLE HAD SOME WATER, AND SOME PEOPLE DIDN'T.

AFTER TWO DAYS AND ONE NIGHT, THROUGH THE WAGON I COULD SEE...
...BARBED WIRE,
VORSICHT
Hochspannung
Lebensgefahr
ELECTRIC FENCES,
SS MEN WITH DOGS.
GGRRR
GGRR
GGRR

WE HAD ARRIVED IN BIRKENAU, AUSCHWITZ.

THE SS MEN SAID,
Men on one side.
Women and children on the other side.
WE MADE TWO LONG LINES.
DOCTOR MENGELE HAPPENED TO BE ON THE SELECTION PLATFORM.
HE POINTED A FINGER TO THE LEFT OR TO THE RIGHT.
TO THE LEFT WENT CHILDREN, MOTHERS WITH CHILDREN, ELDERLY MEN.

I'D NOTICED A LOT OF THE PEOPLE WHO WERE CHOSEN TO GO TO THE RIGHT WERE FITTER MEN.
I KNEW THAT WAS A GOOD THING WITH THE NAZIS.
IF THEY DIDN'T NEED YOU, THEN THAT WAS IT.
AAHHH!
THEN SUDDENLY, THEY TRIED TO TAKE A CHILD AWAY FROM HER MOTHER.
My daughter!
AND SHE STARTED SCREAMING, AND THE NAZI SS MEN RAN TOWARD HER.

AS THEY RAN THERE, I DECIDED TO GO OVER TO THE RIGHT.

I WAS VERY LUCKY. ALL THE PEOPLE THAT WENT TO THE LEFT-HAND SIDE WENT TO THE GAS CHAMBERS. THEY GASSED THEM AND THEN BURNED THEIR BODIES.

WE WALKED INTO A PLACE CALLED THE SAUNA...
...A BRICK-BUILT BUILDING IN BIRKENAU.

WE WERE TOLD TO LEAVE ALL OUR CLOTHING ON THE FLOOR.

I HAD SIX PHOTOGRAPHS OF MY FAMILY...

THEY WERE TAKEN AWAY, AND THAT'S THE LAST TIME I'VE EVER HAD A PHOTOGRAPH OF MY FAMILY.

I HAD MY HEAD SHAVED.
AND FROM THERE, WE WENT INTO THE NEXT ROOM AND WERE GIVEN OUR UNIFORMS.
STRIPED SUITS. MINE WAS BIG ON ME, SO I PULLED IT UP.

THEY DIDN'T GIVE US ANY BATHS OR SHOWERS. WE SOON STARTED HAVING PROBLEMS WITH LICE.
LICE WALKED ALL OVER US. ITCHY, YES, VERY ITCHY. THEY LIVE ON YOUR SKIN.
WE WERE A THOUSAND MEN IN A BARRACK.
THREE BUNKS HIGH...
...TEN PEOPLE ON A BUNK.

WE SLEPT ON THE BOARDS. THERE WAS NO STRAW, THERE WERE NO COVERS.

PEOPLE SNORED, PEOPLE MOANED, PEOPLE DIED NEXT TO YOU.

AT 5:30 IN THE MORNING, THEY WOKE US UP AND THEY ALLOWED US TO GO TO THE WASHROOM.

IN THE WASHROOM THERE WERE ABOUT FIVE BUCKETS OF WATER.

AND YOU JUST DIPPED YOUR HANDS...
...WASHED YOUR EYES...
...AND THAT WAS IT.
I WAS JUST SKIN AND BONES, BECAUSE THEY DIDN'T FEED US.
I'm so hungry!
THEY GAVE US A SMALL PIECE OF BREAD IN THE MORNING, WITH SOME BLACK COFFEE MADE OF BURNT WHEAT.

AND LUNCHTIME, WE GOT SOME WATERY SOUP WITH A FEW LEAVES SWIMMING IN IT AND THAT WAS IT.
LIVE ON THAT FOR MONTHS AND YEARS, GOING ON, YOU'RE JUST LIKE A SKELETON.
YOUR MIND CAN'T THINK PROPERLY, YOUR BODY IS WEAK, YOU'RE STARVING ALL THE TIME.
YOU THINK ABOUT FOOD ALL THE TIME. YOU CAN'T HELP BUT THINK ABOUT IT.

IN AUSCHWITZ, I WAS TATTOOED. I'VE GOT A NUMBER...
B7608
...ON MY LEFT ARM. IT'S STILL THERE NOW, AND I JUST CAN'T TAKE IT OFF.
I'VE LOST 81 PEOPLE FROM MY FAMILY.
I ONLY FOUND MY SISTER TWO YEARS AFTER THE WAR.
HOW COULD I SAY HOW IT CHANGED ME?
SPLASH
SPLASH
SPLASH
I'LL NEVER FORGET WHAT I WENT THROUGH.

AREK SURVIVED SEVERAL GHETTOS AND CONCENTRATION CAMPS BETWEEN THE AGES OF 11 AND 16. ONLY 40 PEOPLE FROM AREK'S HOMETOWN SURVIVED THE WAR.

What Happened Next?

After the war ended, Heinz married Thea. They had two sons. Both sons went to Oxford, the first members of the family ever to go to college. Heinz had a successful career as head of a leading housing organization.

Trude did very well at school and won a scholarship to college. She went on to become a medical biochemist and university lecturer. Trude is still searching for information about what happened to her mother.

Ruth married, had five children, and became a successful secondary school teacher. She continues to speak about her experiences in schools in England and in Israel, and is committed to keeping the memory of the Holocaust alive.

Martin's mother and sister also survived the war. None of Martin's relatives in Poland were so fortunate—22 of them in total were rounded up and shot by the Nazis. Martin went on to become an eminent scientist and a university lecturer.

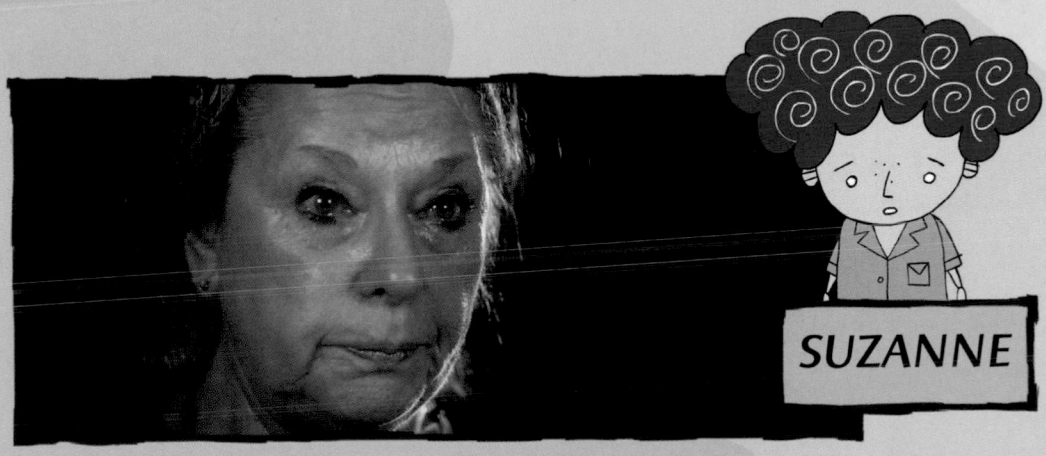

It took Suzanne many years to learn and understand what happened to her during the war. She now has two sons and several grandchildren. Madame Collomb, Suzanne's rescuer, has been recognized for her bravery at the Yad Vashem Holocaust Museum in Israel.

Many years passed before Arek could talk fully about his experiences of the war. He subsequently wrote a book about what happened. Today he gives talks and shows groups around Auschwitz-Birkenau. He has been given an award by Queen Elizabeth II for his work.

Glossary

air-raid shelter *The place where people hide from bombs being dropped from airplanes.*

arrondissement *An administrative district (neighborhood) of certain large cities in France, including Paris.*

barracks *A building or group of buildings used as basic living quarters.*

Blitz *A period of intense German air raids on British cities, from September 1940 to May 1941.*

British Ambassador *The head of the British Embassy, who represents his or her government in a foreign country.*

chenille *Thick cloth.*

civil servant *Someone who works in a government office.*

concentration camps *Purpose-built camps used by the Nazis to imprison huge numbers of Jewish people, as well as others including communists, homosexuals, and church leaders.*

curfew *The time period when people have to stay indoors or risk breaking the law.*

Czechoslovakia *A country that used to exist in eastern Europe and which was divided into the Czech Republic and Slovakia in 1993.*

deportation *Being forced to leave your home and your country.*

digs *Rented room or rooms to live in.*

embassy *The building where an ambassador and his officials live and work in a foreign country.*

enemy aliens *Foreigners who were living in Britain when the Second World War broke out and who came from countries that were now at war with Britain.*

foster parents *People who act as a child's parents in place of their own parents.*

gas chamber *An airtight room that can be filled with poisonous gas in order to poison the people inside.*

Gestapo *Secret police who played a large role in persecuting Jewish people.*

ghettos *Overcrowded districts within cities, designed to separate Jewish people from the rest of the population.*

Hitler, Adolf (1889–1945) *The political leader of Germany from 1933 to 1945 and the head of the Nazi Party.*

Hitler Youth *German youth group, controlled by the Nazi Party.*

Holocaust *The systematic murder of six million Jewish people by the Nazi Party.*

Home Office *The part of the British government responsible for law and order, security, and immigration.*

inferior *Feeling that you are not as good as someone else.*

internment camp *A camp where enemy aliens were kept captive for political reasons.*

Jew *A member of the Jewish community who may also follow the religion Judaism.*

Jude *The German word for a Jewish person.*

Kindertransport *(Children's Transport) The name given to the rescue efforts that brought approximately 10,000 children to Great Britain as refugees from Nazi persecution between 1938 and 1940.*

kipper *A smoked herring; a type of fish.*

Kristallnacht *The anti-Jewish riots that occurred on November 9th and 10th, 1938. Thousands of Jews were arrested and their homes, synagogues, and businesses were burnt down or wrecked.*

marionettes *Puppets whose legs, feet, and head are moved by pulling on strings.*

Mengele, Dr. Josef (1911–1979) *Nazi doctor, member of the SS, who worked at Auschwitz-Birkenau, performing cruel operations and other medical procedures as part of his medical research.*

Nazis *Short for the National Socialist German Workers' (Nazi) Party. This was a German political party that existed from 1920 to 1945.*

Nuremberg Laws *Laws passed by the Nazi Party in 1935 that stripped Jewish people of German citizenship.*

occupied/occupation *From June 1940 to late August 1944, Germans governed (occupied) northern and western France, including Paris.*

pantry *A cupboard or small room in a house used for storing food.*

peers *People of the same age.*

Polenaktion *In October 1938, 12,000 Polish Jews living in Germany were deported—expelled—from Germany.*

Red Cross *An international organization that cares for people suffering because of war or natural disasters.*

Reisepass *The German word for passport.*

salvation *Being saved from danger.*

selection platform *New arrivals at concentration camps were processed by officials standing on a raised platform and were selected to die immediately or be sent to work.*

self-sufficient *Being able to provide for all your needs and not rely on help from anyone else.*

SS *Short for Schutzstaffel, the German word for defense squadron. This military unit of the Nazi Party served as Adolf Hitler's bodyguards and became a major security force for the Nazi Party in concentration camps.*

Star of David *A six-pointed star that is a symbol of the Jewish religion.*

swastika *An ancient symbol that was used by the German Nazi Party.*

synagogue *Jewish place of worship.*

testimony *A spoken statement, often in a court of law, saying what someone believes to be true.*

transport/transported *The term used to describe rounding up Jewish people and putting them on trains to travel to concentration camps, death camps, and work camps.*

visa *An official stamp or mark put into a passport by a government official which gives someone the right to enter a foreign country or leave their own country.*

Timeline

January 30, 1933
Adolf Hitler is appointed Chancellor, the German head of government. He leads the National Socialist German Workers' (Nazi) Party.

March 1933
The Nazis open the first concentration camps where they imprison anyone who opposes their ideas.

1933–1935
The German government gradually introduces laws that isolate Jewish people from the rest of society and limit their freedom and opportunities. They use propaganda, such as speeches and newspaper articles, to spread lies about Jewish people, burn books by Jewish authors, and encourage people to boycott Jewish shops and businesses. Jewish people are banned from mixing with non-Jewish people in parks, swimming pools, orchestras, clubs, and playgrounds. Many Jewish children and students are forced to leave school or university.

September 15, 1935
The Nuremberg Laws take away German citizenship from Jews.

March 13, 1938
German troops march into Austria.

October 1938
Polenaktion: 12,000 Polish Jews living in Germany are deported (expelled) from Germany.

November 9-10, 1938
Kristallnacht: Anti-Jewish riots occur throughout Germany, Austria, and Sudetenland (disputed land in Czechoslovakia). Synagogues, Jewish homes, and businesses are destroyed by fire or have their windows smashed. Thousands of Jewish people are arrested and kept in camps for several weeks and others are murdered. Life for Jewish people becomes considerably more difficult.

November/December 1938
Jewish children are only allowed to attend separate Jewish schools.

December 1938–1940
Kindertransport rescue missions bring 10,000 Jewish children to Britain. The children have to be under 17 years old, travel without their parents, and have arrangements in place where either individuals or organizations are prepared to pay for their needs in Great Britain.

March 15, 1939
Germany invades Czechoslovakia.

September 1, 1939
Germany invades Poland.

September 3, 1939
Britain and France declare war on Germany. Prime Minister Neville Chamberlain announces that Britain is at war with Germany using a radio broadcast. Enemy aliens are put in internment camps or placed under surveillance.

September 17, 1939
The Soviet Union invades Poland. By the end of the month, Germany and the Soviet Union have divided Poland between themselves.

September 21, 1939
From this date, Polish Jews are ordered to live in ghettos.

October 1939
The Nazis begin to deport Jewish people from Austria and Poland to camps.

November 1939
Polish Jews are forced to wear a Star of David on their chests or as an armband.

1940
Prime Minister Neville Chamberlain resigns, to be replaced by Winston Churchill.

1940
In Germany, Jewish people have their telephones removed; they had already had their radios confiscated in 1939.

April 30, 1940
The Lodz ghetto in Poland is the first ghetto to be sealed off behind guarded defenses.

April-June 1940
Germany invades Denmark, Norway, Luxembourg, the Netherlands, and Belgium. France signs an armistice agreement whereby the Germans occupy the northern half of the country, including Paris, and southern France is governed by the Vichy French government.

July 1940
French Jews are expelled to southern France.

September 1940–May 1941
The Blitz: a succession of intense bombing raids by the German air force on British cities, including London and Coventry.

1941
Jewish people are forbidden from using public telephones or leaving the country. Jewish people from across German-occupied territory are forcibly removed to ghettos or camps.

June 1941
Germany invades the Soviet Union. German troops are ordered to kill all Jewish people they come across.

September 1941
All Jewish people over the age of 6 have to wear a yellow Star of David with "Jew" written on it.

December 1941
Japan attacks Pearl Harbor, leading to the U.S. declaring war against Germany, Japan, and Italy.

1941–1942
The Nazis open six extermination or death camps in Poland, including Auschwitz-Birkenau.

January 1942
Nazi leaders meet in Berlin to discuss how to organize the mass murder of the Jewish people, known as the "Final Solution."

February 1942
Gas chambers begin operation at Auschwitz-Birkenau, murdering Jewish people.

June 1942
The German government closes all Jewish schools.

July 1942
Around 74,000 French Jews are transported to death camps.

1942–1943
German forces deport Jewish people from ghettos to camps, where thousands are forced into gas chambers and killed, or worked to death in forced labor camps.

May 1943
Dr. Mengele begins work at Auschwitz-Birkenau.

May–July 1944
Jews are deported from Hungary to camps, such as Auschwitz-Birkenau.

June 6, 1944
D-Day: U.S., British, Canadian, and French forces (and other Allied troops) invade German-held Normandy in France. Slowly they fight their way across Europe.

June 22, 1944
The Soviet Union launches a major attack on German forces in eastern Europe and pushes across Poland, uncovering evidence of many concentration camps.

Late 1944–spring 1945
As the German army retreats from the Soviet army, the SS forces prisoners in concentration camps to march west, sometimes traveling in train carriages, back to Germany. Known as "death marches," hundreds of thousands of Jewish people die.

January 1945
Soviet troops liberate prisoners remaining in Auschwitz-Birkenau.

1945
As British and U.S. troops and those fighting alongside them fight their way across Europe and into Germany, they come across horribly overcrowded camps, full of prisoners on the verge of death. Many prisoners are so weak that they die.

April 30, 1945
Adolf Hitler commits suicide.

May 8, 1945
Victory in Europe (VE) Day. Germany surrenders and the Second World War in Europe comes to an end.

Summer 1945 onward
Displaced persons camps are established across Austria, Italy, and Germany for people rescued from Nazi camps and other refugees. At first, conditions are poor, but gradually they improve and aid agencies help people to trace surviving relatives and start to rebuild their lives.

August 1945
Atomic bombs are dropped on Hiroshima and Nagasaki in Japan, killing between 150,000–300,000 people. Japan surrenders and the Second World War comes to an end.

Index

air raids **56–60**
British Embassy **37–38**
Chamberlain, Neville **42–43**
Churchill, Winston **16**
concentration camps
  Auschwitz-Birkenau **29, 78–89**
  Dachau **14**
  Sered **30**
Czechoslovakia **20–25, 34–39**
death marches **31**
education **8–9, 20, 63, 69**
enemy aliens **16–17**
France **62–74**
gas chambers **81**
Germany **6–15, 18, 34, 38–39, 43, 46–51, 54**
Gestapo **14**
Hitler, Adolf **22, 34**
Hitler Youth **8**
internment **17–18**
Kindertransport **55**
Kristallnacht **13**
Mengele, Josef **79**
Nuremberg Laws **7**
outbreak of Second World War **15–16, 41–44**
Poland **29, 35, 42, 46–47, 49, 51–55, 76–89**
Polenaktion **46–54**
synagogues **10, 12**
transports **29–30**
visas **15, 38**

Websites

BBC Learning Children of the Holocaust animations
Watch the animations that inspired this book, and interviews with the survivors themselves.
bbc.co.uk/programmes/p01zx5g7

Fettle Animation
The multi-award-winning animation company behind this project.
fettleanimation.com

Holocaust Survivors' Friendship Association
Find out more about the people in this book and their ongoing educational work.
holocaustlearning.org

6 Million Plus
Organization in Yorkshire, UK, that explores the connection between the Holocaust and the experience of persecuted minorities today.
6millionplus.org

Holocaust Memorial Day Trust
The charity that promotes and supports Holocaust Memorial Day on January 27th every year.
hmd.org.uk

The National Holocaust Centre and Museum
Museum in Nottingham, UK, that hosts daily talks by Holocaust survivors, plus an exhibition designed especially for younger children.
nationalholocaustcentre.net

Anne Frank Trust
Resources to help children understand the Holocaust.
annefrank.org.uk

Imperial War Museum London
Award-winning permanent Holocaust exhibition.
iwm.org.uk/events/the-holocaust-exhibition

Yad Vashem
Museum and Holocaust research institute in Israel.
yadvashem.org

Wiener Library London
Library for the study of the Holocaust and genocide.
wienerlibrary.co.uk

International Tracing Service
Center for research on the Holocaust, documenting what happened to victims of the Nazis.
its-arolsen.org

USC Shoah Foundation
Archive of interviews with Holocaust survivors and educational resources.
sfi.usc.edu

United States Holocaust Memorial Museum
U.S. memorial to the Holocaust. Features an exhibition designed for young people and a Hall of Remembrance.
ushmm.org

Auschwitz-Birkenau Memorial and Museum
Visit the former concentration camp and tour its museum.
auschwitz.org/en/